DK Watch me grow

Penguin

LONDON, NEW YORK, M
MELBOURNE, and DELHI

Written and edited by Lisa Magloff
Designed by Sonia Whillock,
Mary Sandberg, and Pilar Morales

Publishing Manager Sue Leonard
Managing Art Editor Clare Shedden
Jacket Design Simon Oon
Picture Researcher Sarah Stewart-Richardson
Production Shivani Pandey
DTP Designer Almudena Díaz

First published in Great Britain in 2004 by
Dorling Kindersley Limited
80 Strand, London WC2R 0RL

A Penguin Company

ISBN 1-4053-0385-9

Colour reproduction by Media, Development and Printing, Ltd.
Printed and bound by South China Printing Co. Ltd. China

see our complete catalogue at
www.dk.com

Contents

Come dive with us and watch us GROW!

I'm a penguin

I live in the Antarctic
where it is very cold.
I am a bird but I do not fly.
Instead, I swim in the
ocean to find my food.

Penguins use their
flippers like wings
to help them move
under the water.

Long, sharp
claws help the
penguin to
grip the ice
and snow.

The penguin's ears are underneath this orange and yellow fur.

All together now
When they are on land, these Emperor penguins live together in a big group called a colony.

Turn the page and find out how our lives began...

My mum and dad

My mum and dad spend most of the year apart at sea. In April, when it is time to mate, they come onto land. They recognize each other by their cries.

Penguin facts

🐧 Penguins return to the same colony every year.

🐧 There are only about 40 colonies of Emperor penguins in the world, and about 400,000 adults.

🐧 The adult penguins are about the height of a 3 or 4 year old child.

Making noise
Emperor penguins have very loud voices. This is important, since they recognize each other by their voice, not by sight.

This is my dad.

Eeearreekkk...

This is my mum.

Dad is left in charge

After Mum lays my egg, she gives it to Dad, who tucks it under his pouch. Now it's time for Mum to go off and find food while Dad keeps my egg warm and safe.

Father penguins don't eat while the mothers are away.

Feather bed
Look closely at this picture. Can you see the egg sitting snugly under its dad's fluffy feathers?

Standing still

Father penguins have to move slowly and carefully so they don't drop their eggs.

It takes Mum days to reach the sea.

Foot-powered travel

Female penguins scoot off to the sea by sliding on their tummies, since this is quicker than walking. They spend the winter feeding in the sea, then return in the spring just before their egg hatches.

It's time for me to hatch

Dad has been keeping me warm for two months. Now Mum returns and he gives her my egg. I will be born in Mum's pouch, while Dad goes to eat.

crack, crack, crack...

...here I come.

Free at last!

Breaking out
The chick uses a hard spot on its beak, called an egg tooth, to peck its way slowly out of the egg. It can take three days to hatch out.

Feather care

The chick's downy feathers are soft and warm, but they are not waterproof. Mum helps keep them clean and fluffy.

I'm two days old.

Mum's big toes lift the chick off the frozen ground and keep it warm.

My mum and dad both look after me

After I am born, Mum and Dad take turns feeding me and keeping me safe and warm.

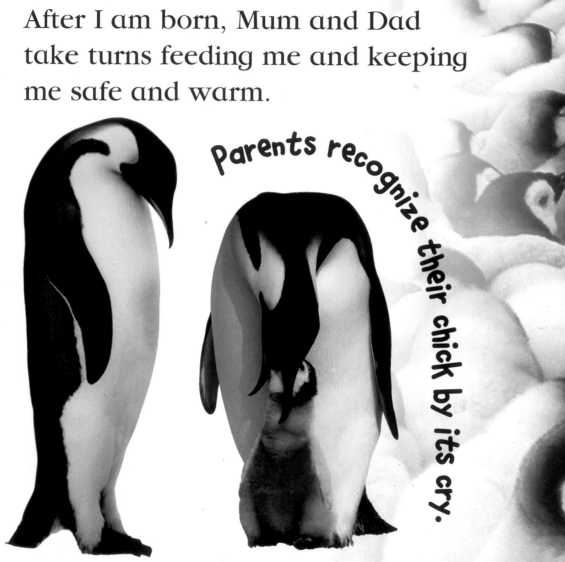

Parents recognize their chick by its cry.

Spitting up dinner
The penguin parents store food in their stomachs and then spit it up for the chick.

While their parents gather food, the chicks huddle together in groups called crèches.

Chick facts
. . . .

🐧 The chicks only eat about 16 meals in the five months it takes them to grow up.

🐧 Huddling together keeps the chicks warm.

My adult feathers grow in

After five months, I am starting to grow my adult, waterproof feathers. This means I'll be able to swim and find my own food.

Squawk squaaark!! Feed me!

This penguin is as big as his father, but he can't feed himself yet.

Waterproofing

It takes the penguin a few weeks to lose its baby feathers and grow adult feathers. This is called fledging.

All change

Adult penguins also grow new feathers each year as the old ones wear out.

My first swim

Now that I have my waterproof feathers, I'm ready to start swimming and hunting for my own fish dinner.

Penguins use their flippers to help them move under water.

16

These penguins are waiting in line to dive into the icy cold water.

Penguin dinner
Penguins eat many kinds of food, like fish and shellfish, but their favourite foods are squid and small shrimp called krill.

Krill

Squid

My first fishing lesson

It's time for me to learn how to dive
and how to catch tasty fish to eat.
I learn how to catch my own dinner
by watching the adult penguins.

The penguins follow
shoals of fish. When
they catch a fish, they
swallow it whole.

A flying finish

The only time that Emperor penguins fly is when they leave the water. They leap out and make a belly flop onto the ice.

These mackerel are a tasty meal.

Emperor penguins can spend up to 20 minutes underwater on one breath.

The circle of life goes round and round

Now you know how I turned into a grown-up penguin.

Bye bye, see you next winter.

My friends from around the world

This Little Blue penguin is only 25 cm (12 in) tall.

The Gentoo penguin is the only penguin that raises two chicks at one time.

The Humbolt penguin lives in warm countries such as South Africa.

My favourite food is squid.

This is a Chinstrap penguin. Can you see how it got its name? It lives on an Antarctic island.

My friends and I all have black and white feathers, and some of us have amazing hairstyles too.

The Macaroni penguin is the most common penguin.

Rockhopper penguins move by hopping from rock to rock.

I am about 1 metre (3 ft) tall.

I'm a yellow- eyed penguin.

King penguins look a lot like Emperor penguins, but they are smaller and have more orange colour.

Penguin facts

🐧 Penguins can drink both saltwater and freshwater.

🐧 Penguins have bristles on their tongues that keep slippery seafood from getting away.

🐧 Penguins only live in the Southern hemisphere.

Glossary

Flippers
The wings of the penguin. They help the penguin swim in water.

Pouch
A flap of fur the baby penguin snuggles under to keep warm.

Colony
A group of penguins that lives together in one place.

Crèche
A group of baby penguins that is looked after by one adult.

Hatch
When the baby penguin pecks its way out of its egg.

Fledge
When a penguin grows its adult, waterproof feathers.

Acknowledgements
The publisher would like to thank the following for their kind permission to reproduce their photographs:
(Key: a=above; c=centre; b=below; l=left; r=right; t=top)
1 Corbis: Tim Davis bkgnd; Royalty Free Images: Corbis. 2-3 Getty Images: Tim Davis. 2 Corbis: Kevin Schafer tr. 3 Corbis: Wolfgang Kaehler bl; Zefa Picture Library: H. Reinhard c. 4-5 Corbis: Tim Davis. 4 Bruce Coleman Ltd: Johnny Johnson cl; FLPA - Images of Nature: F Lanting/ Minden Pictures bc. Getty Images: Pete Oxford r. 5 Alamy Images: Fritz Poelking/ Elvele Images tr. Corbis: Clive Druett tl. 6-7 ImageState/Pictor: David Tipling c, t; Corbis: Tim Davis b. 7 Alamy Images: Galen Rowell/ Mountain Light. 8-9 FLPA - Images of Nature: Frans Lanting. 8 Alamy Images: Paul Gunning l; Nature Picture Library Ltd: Doug Allan br. 9 Science Photo Library: Doug Allan t. 10-11 FLPA - Images of Nature: Frans Lanting/ Minden Pictures. 10 DK Images: Jane Burton tl, cr; Sea World/ San Diego Zoo: br. 12-13 FLPA - Images of Nature: Frans Lanting/ Minden Pictures. 12 Bruce Coleman Ltd: Hans Reinhard c; FLPA - Images of Nature: K Wothe/ Minden Pictures l. 14-15 Corbis: John Conrad. 15 ImageState/Pictor: Hummel/ Fotonatura; FLPA - Images of nature: C Carvalho tr. 16 Bruce Coleman Ltd: Johnny Johnson bl; Corbis: Tim Davis tl; Robert Harding Picture Library: Johnny Johnson br. 17 Corbis: Tim Davis t; DK Images: Frank Greenaway bc; Harry Taylor br. 18-19 Corbis: Stuart Westmorland. 18 National Geographic Image Collection: Bill Curtsinger. 19 Nature Picture Library Ltd: Doug Allan c; Pete Oxford tr; Oxford Scientific Films: Doug Allan bkg. 20 Bruce Coleman Ltd: Dr. Eckart Pott tl; Johnny Johnson c; Corbis: Tim Davis clb, crb, bcr; DK Images: Jane Burton tc, tr; Oxford Scientific Films: Doug Allan bcl; Royalty Free Images: Corbis cr; Sea World/ San Diego Zoo: trb; Getty Images: Pete Oxford cr. 21 N.H.P.A.: B & C Alexander. 22-23 FLPA - Images of Nature: Gerald Lacz. 22 Howard Porter: Daniel Zupanc tr; FLPA - Images of Nature: David Hosking bl; Tui De Roy/ Minden Pictures b; Oxford Scientific Films: Gerald L. Kooyman tr. 23 Alamy Images: Bryan & Cherry Alexander br; Ardea London Ltd: cr; Peter Steyn tr; FLPA - Images of Nature: Terry Andrewartha tr. 24 Bruce Coleman Ltd: Johnny Johnson tl; Corbis: Fritz Polking/ Frank Lane Picture Agency cr; ImageState/Pictor: Hummel/ Fotonatura br; Oxford Scientific Films: Doug Allan cr; Sea World/ San Diego Zoo: bl.
All other images © Dorling Kindersley
For further information see: www.dkimages.com